Ki

This i
or re
Boro
befo
star
is r
re
k

Is our Weather getting WORSE?

John Townsend

Published 2009 by
A & C Black Publishers Ltd.
36 Soho Square, London, W1D 3QY
www.acblack.com

ISBN HB 978-1-4081-0854-3
      PB 978-1-4081-1294-6

Series consultant: Gill Matthews

This book is produced using paper that is made from wood grown in managed, sustainable
forests. It is natural, renewable and recyclable. The logging and manufacturing processes
conform to the environmental regulations of the country of origin.

Produced for A & C Black by Calcium.
Printed and bound in China by C&C Offset Printing Co.

All the internet addresses given in this book were correct at the time of going to press.
The author and publishers regret any inconvenience caused if addresses have changed
or sites have ceased to exist, but can accept no responsibility for any such changes.

Acknowledgements
The publishers would like to thank the following for their kind permission to reproduce their
photographs:
Cover: Shutterstock. **Pages:** Alamy: Neil McAllister 9; Corbis: Reuters 19; Dreamstime:
Jhaz 5; Fotolia: ch'lu 11; Getty: Topical Press Agency 6; Istockphoto: John Pitcher 13, Yarinca
20, Yenwen Lu 4; NASA/GSFC/Jacques Descloitres, MODIS Land Rapid Response Team 17;
Science Photo Library: David Hay Jones 7, Hank Morgan 18; Shutterstock: Lars Christensen 10,
Jack Dagley Photography 8, Evan Meyer 15, Konstantin Mironov 12, Ragnarock 21.
Illustrations: Geoff Ward 14.

CONTENTS

IT NEVER USED TO BE LIKE THIS!

Everyone talks about the weather because it affects our daily lives. Many people say it is getting worse. This book tries to find out if that is true.

Cold winters – hot summers?

Older people sometimes say that winters used to be much colder and summers far less wet. They may even say they did not see floods and strong winds during their childhood. This makes it seem as if weather used to be better long ago. Can that really be true?

Wind, rain, snow, cold, and sunshine affect what we do and how we feel.

What do the experts say?

People who study the weather are called meteorologists. Some of them say the weather is not really getting worse but it is just different. They say the weather has kept changing over hundreds of years.

"The latest research shows that some extreme events are already growing. The trend is set to continue. Our changing climate is having a real impact, with warmer nights and hotter days in the future."
UK Met Office (2008)

Some scientists say our weather is changing more quickly now than ever before. Our weather may become more extreme in the future.

Weather and climate

The weather is what happens at a particular place at a particular time, including the temperature, sunlight, wind, and rainfall. The **climate** is "the bigger picture" that shows a larger area in less detail.

HOW CAN WE TELL?

What was the weather like hundreds of years ago? Old newspapers, books, pictures, and modern-day scientific work show that the weather used to be different.

Long ago winters
The winters in London, 200 years ago, were often much colder than today. The River Thames used to freeze over.

Seas used to freeze more often, too. In 1658, a Swedish army was able to march across the frozen sea to Denmark. In 1780, New York harbour froze over, so people could walk from Manhattan to Staten Island.

People used to skate across the frozen River Thames.

Ancient weather

By drilling into the ground and taking out a **core of ice** or mud, scientists can tell a lot about the seasons long ago. The deeper layers of a core are many years older than layers near the surface. Scientists study the layers of ice and mud to learn about ancient weather.

Types of pollen found in the layers of mud show changes in plant life and the weather over the last few thousand years.

A scientist drills deep into Arctic ice to find out what the weather was like hundreds of years ago.

Clues in the mud

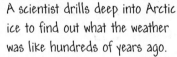

- Pollen from tropical plants – show the weather was once warmer in the area.
- Fossils of desert creatures – show the weather was once hotter and drier.
- Layers of sand – show that an area was once a hot desert.

WEATHER RECORDS

There are some scary weather records out there. Did you know that the highest gust of wind recorded on the ground in the UK was over 225 kmh (140 mph)? It was at Fraserburgh, Aberdeenshire, on 13 February 1989.

Dangerous weather

In 1999, America had a heatwave that killed more than 185 people. Soon after, in Iowa, huge thunderstorms dropped golf ball-sized hail and over 30 cm (12 in) of rain fell. Many roads were flooded and had to close.

Hailstones as big as golf balls fell in Iowa in 1999.

Is the weather getting worse today?

For over 100 years, meteorologists have kept details of the weather around the country every day. This detail is called weather **data**. It can tell us if our weather is getting worse.

Weather data record sheet

Place: UK	Date: 8/5/1915
Coldest temperature (min)	12° C (53°F)
Hottest temperature (max)	23° C (73°F)
Average rainfall (rain)	3 mm (0.1 in)
Average sunshine (sun)	118 mins

A meteorologist records rainfall data from a rain gauge.

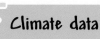

Climate data

Climate change is the shift in long-term weather patterns. By looking at data from around the world, meteorologists can tell it's getting warmer – and that can make a big difference.

Data can be added together for the whole year. This gives important information about climate.

Climate data record sheet

Place: USA   **Date: 1915**

Average temperature   16°C (60°F)

Total average rainfall for year   1.353 mm (53 in)

Total average sunshine   1,258 hours

RECORD BREAKERS – IS IT GETTING WETTER?

Some people complain that we get far more rain than we used to. Others disagree. They say it only seems like it because we go out more these days. Who do you think is right?

Rainfall records

Greatest rainfall	Amount	Place
In a year:	2,644 cm (1,041 in)	Assam, India; August 1880
In a day:	187 cm (73.55 in)	Indian Ocean; 15 March 1952
In a minute:	3.1 cm (1.2 in)	Unionville, Maryland, USA; July 1956

Floods

Some of the worst floods in Britain were over 50 years ago. This is what a woman in Suffolk said about the rising water in her house in 1953:

"We went to the window, but the water was coming up very fast. It was nearly up to the windowsill. Everything was floating – the table, chairs and sideboard. The dog was standing on the armchair, bobbing about like a cork."

Floods are nothing new, but should we expect more record-breaking amounts of rain?

Record-breakers

- June 1998, Boston, USA, broke a 117-year-old record for its heavy rainfall.
- July 2007, Britain had its wettest summer. Homes were washed away and some people drowned.
- June 2008, Hong Kong recorded the heaviest downpour since records began – 145.5 mm (nearly 6 in) of rain fell in one hour.

Bad floods soon bring towns to a standstill.

Not all record-breakers have taken place in the summer. In February 1998, Santa Barbara in California, had 56 cm (22 in) of rainfall, making it California's wettest month on record.

GLOBAL WARMING: THE BIGGER PICTURE

Meteorologists' reports suggest the world is warming up. We call this **global warming**. In fact, some scientists think that when babies born today reach 80 years old, the world will be 3.5°C (6°F) warmer than it is now.

Record temperatures
During the summer of 1998, the USA had record temperatures. More than 140 people died from the heat. In 2003, almost 15,000 people died during a heatwave in France.

Melting roads!
In July 2006, it was so hot in parts of England that roads melted. In one school classroom temperatures reached 32°C (89°F) and parents were told that the school would have to close.

Forest fires can also be a big problem in very hot summers. They can destroy miles of trees and wildlife.

Melting ice and polar bears

Scientists say temperatures in the Arctic have risen by 5°C (9°F) over the last 40 years. That is bad news for Arctic wildlife. As the Arctic warms up, snow caves where seals shelter are melting. Baby seals die from the cold winds. Polar bears eat seals but now their food is disappearing.

Melting arctic ice is threatening the polar bear's way of life.

"For anyone who has wondered how global warming will affect polar bears, the answer is simple - they die." Richard Steiner, University of Alaska

Sizzling world records

Even though the world is warming up, the hottest temperatures recorded are nearly 100 years ago.

Place	Date	Temperature
Death Valley, USA	10 July, 1913	56.7°C (133°F)
Libya, Africa	13 September, 1922	58°C (136°F)

IS IT REALLY US?

Many scientists say people are producing too many gases that warm up the Earth. We call this our **carbon footprint**, and it is turning the Earth into a great big greenhouse.

Greenhouse gases

Greenhouses work by trapping heat from the Sun. The glass of a greenhouse lets in light but stops heat from escaping. Greenhouse gases, including **carbon dioxide**, in the **atmosphere** act just like the glass in a greenhouse. Sunlight enters the Earth's atmosphere, the Earth warms and heat rises into the atmosphere. Some of the heat escapes up into space. But thick layers of greenhouse gas trap some of the heat which makes the world warmer. This is called the **greenhouse effect**.

Some of the Sun's rays escape the Earth's atmosphere

Gases trapped in Earth's atmosphere keep Earth warm

Some of the Sun's rays are trapped in Earth's atmosphere

Greenhouse gases rise above the Earth and form a "lid" above us. Heat is trapped under the lid, which warms up the planet.

What makes greenhouse gas?

- Plants and animals.
- Smoke from forest fires and volcanoes.
- People burning coal, oil, and forests.

Experiment

You can show how the greenhouse effect works by following this simple experiment.

What to do:

1. Take two jars and put a teaspoon of water in each jar.
2. Put a lid on one of the jars.
3. Place both jars in a sunny spot.
4. After a few hours, check the jars.

Results:

You will see that the open jar has not changed. Some of the water may have "disappeared", but the closed jar will be steamy and hot inside. This is because the **water vapour** could not escape.

What this shows:

The heat from the Sun could not escape from the closed jar. The lid acts just like the layer of greenhouse gas around the Earth.

Power stations that burn coal to make electricity also make a lot of greenhouse gas.

WATER, WATER, EVERYWHERE...

As the Earth gets warmer, ice at the North Pole and South Pole melts. That means more water is dripping into the sea. The oceans grow bigger and warmer, and land is covered by the rising water.

This chart shows how ice at the Arctic is shrinking.

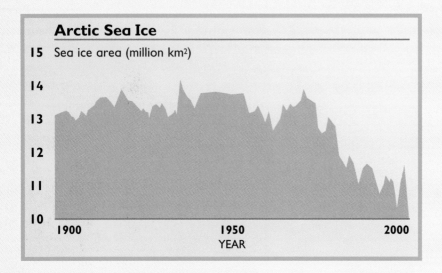

Arctic Sea Ice

Sea ice area (million km²)

YEAR

Scientists keep measuring the ice at the North Pole. In the last 50 years, a tenth has gone. At this rate, soon there will not be much ice left.

Flooded homes

As seas and rivers rise, more people's homes will be flooded. Bigger, warmer oceans also bring more rain. And more rain means more floods.

Roaring hurricanes

Hurricanes bring very strong winds, a lot of rain and more floods. They get their energy from warm water in the oceans. So as the seas get warmer, hurricanes are likely to become more powerful. In fact, according to some experts, hurricanes now happen twice as often as they did 100 years ago.

Flying glass!

This is what one man wrote after a hurricane wrecked his home:

A hurricane seen by a **satellite** from space swirls across the oceans.

"I was asleep but was woken by the roaring wind. As soon as I opened my eyes, the roof above me ripped off. I stared at the swirling black sky as broken glass flew through the air. I ran into the next room where the bed sheets were getting sucked out of the smashed window. I could only hide in a closet and wait for the hurricane to pass."

WHAT MIGHT HAPPEN NEXT?

To find out tomorrow's weather we can check the weather forecast, but what about the climate? The big question is, what will our climate be like in a few years? Scientists are trying to work out what may happen in the future.

Computer data

Scientists use a computer model to work out what the weather will be like at a particular place. By putting in a lot of data about today's weather and what it was like in the past, scientists get the computer to come up with possible answers.

A meteorologist uses a computer model to predict climate changes over the next century.

Global warming

Some countries use huge computers to study global warming. Scientists work out how the Earth's climate keeps changing. They do this by recording temperatures of the air and oceans and by studying clouds and rainfall. They also use satellites to measure ice and snow at the polar ice caps.

Predictions

Scientists predict that by 2100 summers in Britain will be 4°C (7°F) hotter. Summer rainfall could drop by nearly half and winters are likely to get warmer, and wetter with less frost. Germany will have tropical nights and torrential (very heavy) rains. In the United States, it is thought there will be many more powerful storms, summer heatwaves, and warmer winters with more rainfall.

The future

Most experts agree that the Earth is getting warmer and it will keep doing so. For many people round the world, that means the weather is likely to get worse — unless we do something about it.

With more storms and higher sea levels predicted, people who live at the coast will be at greater risk.

WHAT CAN WE DO?

Have you ever left muddy footprints on a clean floor? That is a bit like what we are all doing to our planet. We are leaving behind carbon footprints because things we burn put carbon dioxide into the air, adding to greenhouse gas.

10 easy ways to clean up your carbon footprint

- Only put the amount of water you need in the kettle.
- Only use washers, driers, and dishwashers when you have a full load.
- Do not leave the computer, television or video on standby.
- Switch lights off when you leave a room.
- Have showers instead of baths.
- Use energy-efficient light bulbs.
- Grow your own vegetables and recycle waste in a **compost** heap.
- Buy food that does not have much packaging.
- Walk and cycle when you can.
- Recycle glass bottles, jars, newspapers, magazines, tin cans, and plastic bags.

Save electricity

Much of our electricity is made by burning coal, which gives off greenhouse gases. So the more electricity we use, the bigger our carbon footprint. If we cut back on the electricity we use, we can reduce our carbon footprint.

Plant trees

Did you know that trees take in carbon dioxide from the air? So planting trees is a great way to reduce greenhouse gas.

We can make a difference

There's no doubt that our weather will continue to change. Sometimes it will be for the worse. But think what a difference we can make!

The weather continues to change around the Earth. We all need to try to look after our planet in the future.

GLOSSARY

atmosphere the mass of air and gases that surrounds the Earth

carbon dioxide (CO_2) an important gas used by plants, as well as being a greenhouse gas that helps to keep the Earth warm

carbon footprint a measure of the impact each of us has on the environment, according to how much carbon gas (CO_2) we produce

climate the average temperatures and the average amount of sunlight, wind and rainfall over a period of time

compost a mixture of decayed matter of dead plants and household waste used for enriching soil

core of ice a long tube of ice cut out of all the layers of ice laid down over time

data facts and information as numbers that can be used in a computer

global warming heating of the Earth's atmosphere and oceans

greenhouse effect the warming of the Earth when the Sun's radiation cannot escape into space because of gases in the atmosphere that form a shield

hurricane storm winds of over 112 kmh (70 mph), with rain, thunder, and lightning

satellite a man-made object sent into space to study the Earth

water vapour water in the form of gas or steam that is spread through the atmosphere

FURTHER INFORMATION

Websites

Find out facts about global warming at:
http://tiki.oneworld.net/global_warming/climate_home.html

Discover more about the weather at the UK Met Office website:
www.metoffice.gov.uk/education/primary/students/index.html

Find a carbon detective's kit at:
www.carbondetectives.org.uk/content/home/index.html

Learn more about climate change at:
www.kidsnewsroom.org/climatechange

More information about climate change can be found at:
www.sciencemuseum.org.uk/antenna/climatechange

Books

Changing Weather, Storms by Kelley MacAulay & Bobbie Kalman.
Crabtree Publishing (2006).

Weather World: Photographing the Global Spectacle by Met Office.
David & Charles PLC (2007).

Weather and Climate (Planet Earth) by Jim Pipe. Ticktock Media (2008).

INDEX